TREES

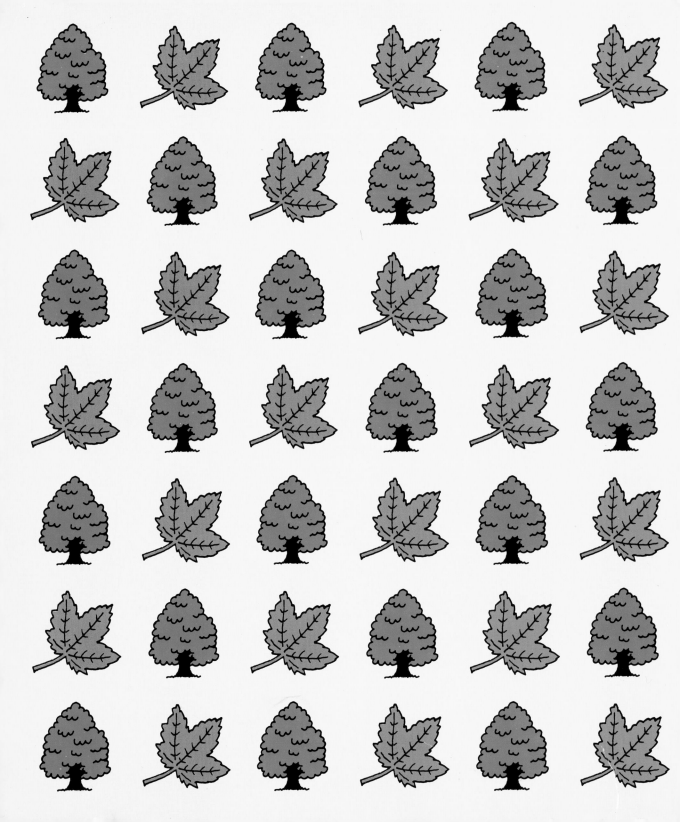

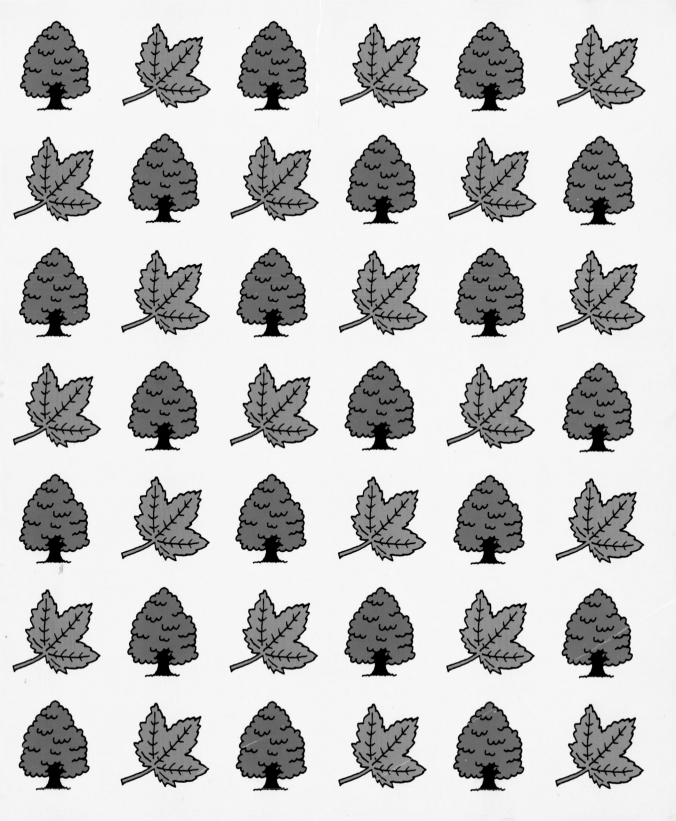

© 1993 Franklin Watts

Franklin Watts, Inc.
95 Madison Avenue
New York, NY 10016

Library of Congress Cataloging-in-Publication Data

Richardson, Joy.
    Trees / by Joy Richardson.
        p. cm. — (Picture science)
    Includes index.
    Summary: An introduction to the world of trees, covering
how they grow, why they lose their leaves, and more.
    ISBN 0-531-14273-6
    1. Trees—Juvenile literature. [1. Trees.] I. Title. II. Series:
Richardson, Joy. Picture science.
QK475.8.R518 1994
582.16—dc20   93-18652
                                                      CIP AC

Editor: Sarah Ridley
Designer: Janet Watson
Illustrator: Angela Owen
Picture researcher: Sarah Moule

Photographs: Bruce Coleman Ltd cover, 13, 14,
27; Frank Lane Picture Agency 10; Natural History
Photographic Agency 7, 9, 16, 19, 20, 23, 24.

Printed in Malaysia

PICTURE SCIENCE

TREES

Joy Richardson

FRANKLIN WATTS

New York • Chicago • London • Toronto • Sydney

Trees at work

Trees grow nearly everywhere on earth.

Trees bind the soil with their roots
and feed it with their leaves.
Trees let out water vapor from
their leaves and help to make rain.

Trees give food, shade, and
shelter to many creatures.

Each year trees grow and
change with the seasons,
as trees have done
for millions of years.

Winter waiting

Many trees lose their leaves each autumn.
They are called deciduous trees.

In winter you can see the sky
through their bare branches.

Old leaves rot into the
soil around the tree roots.
Scattered seeds lie in the ground.

Evergreen trees have tough leaves
that last for several years,
but the trees stop growing
as winter approaches.

Winter is a waiting time.

Beginning with buds

The buds for next year's growth
can be seen on the wintry twigs.

Each tree has its own type of bud.
Beech buds are long and thin.
Ash buds are black and knobby.

Dark scales protect the buds
that are filled with new life.
They contain all the beginnings
of new leaves, flowers, and twigs.

Bursting into life

Horse chestnut buds
have a hard sticky coating.
In the spring the buds swell,
the sticky coating softens, and
the bud scales turn back.

New shoots burst out
and begin to grow rapidly.

Soft green leaves unfold along
each shoot and straighten out.

Flowers grow and bloom
at the end of the shoots.

Flower power

All trees produce flowers.
Flowers make pollen and
catch pollen grains, which
start new seeds.

Fruit trees have flowers with
bright petals to attract
insects that spread the pollen.

The wind blows the pollen from
catkins on willow and hazel trees.
Separate little seed-making
flowers catch pollen.

Many trees are pollinated by the wind.
They do not need beautiful flowers.

Leaf styles

Each type of tree grows
in its own way and has
its own leaf shape.

Sycamore leaves are jagged.
Walnut leaves are smooth.

Beech leaves grow singly.
Ash leaves form pairs.
Horse chestnut leaves fan
out, like fingers on a hand.

As spring turns into summer,
light green leaves grow darker
and the tree fills out.

Sycamore

Beech

Making food

Leaves have a job to do.
They make the tree's food supply.

Each leaf has a layer of
green cells that uses sunlight to
turn water from the ground and
gas from the air into food.

Veins carry water into the leaf
and food out.

Work slows down in the autumn.
The leaves change color
as the sunlight lessens.

The tree seals off the leaf stalks.
This makes the leaves fall.

Needles and cones

Conifers have dark green
needles that survive the winter.
Fir trees have short needles like combs.
Pine trees have long needles in bundles.

Conifers grow their seeds in cones.

Once the seeds have been
pollinated, it may take several
years for the small green cone
to become hard and woody.

When the cone is ready,
the scales open or flake off.
The seeds fall to the ground.

Spreading seeds

Tree seeds may grow inside
scaly cones, juicy fruits, hard nuts,
seed pods, or winged seed cases.

Seeds scatter when they fall to the ground,
are blown by the wind,
or are carried away by animals.

Each tree makes thousands
of seeds a year, but it is hard
for a seed to survive and grow.

Seeds are also gathered and
planted by people,
so that new trees can be
grown where they are needed.

Food for growing

When a seed begins to grow,
it uses its food supply to push
out a root and a leafy shoot.

The root sucks up water.
The leaves begin to make food.
The watery food forms a liquid
called sap, which tiny pipelines
carry up and down the growing tree.

The sap helps new cells to grow.
Each year a new ring of cells grows
around the trunk and branches,
and the old wood hardens.
You can tell a tree's age
by counting the number of rings.

Bark

Bark protects the tree,
like a tough skin.

It keeps the tree safe from
animals and insects and
from the heat of the sun.

Bark can be hard or soft,
smooth or cracked.
Each tree has its own kind of bark.

Beech bark is smooth and gray.
Yew bark is hard and flaky.
Birch bark peels off like paper.

New bark grows on the inside and
pushes out the old crusty bark.

From trees to wood

Oak trees have hard wood
and take a long time to grow.

Pine trees have soft wood
and grow quite quickly.

When trees die or are cut down
after twenty years or two hundred,
it is not the end of the story.

Wood can be used to make
buildings, or furniture, or toys.
It can also be turned into paper.

The wood can be used
for many years to come.

Index

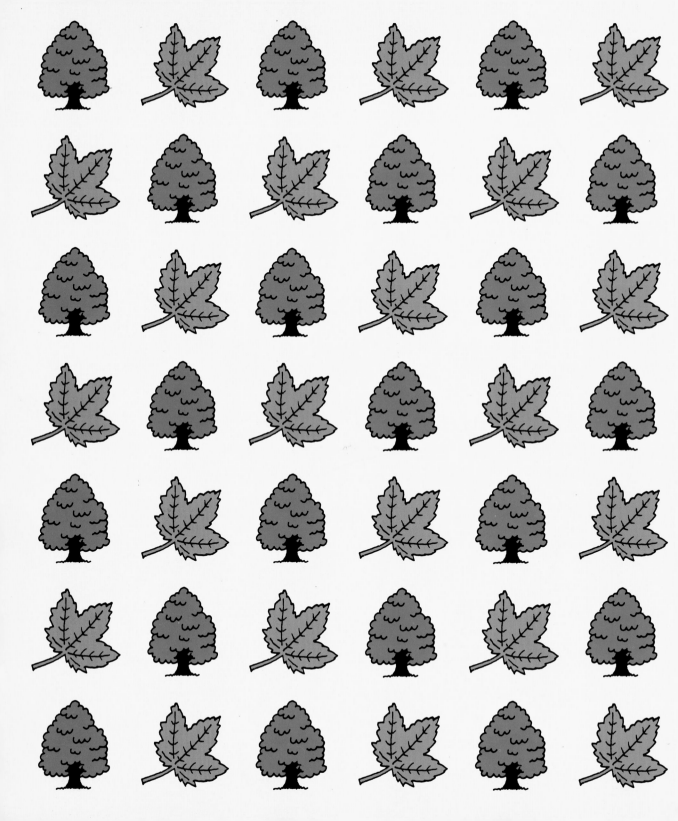

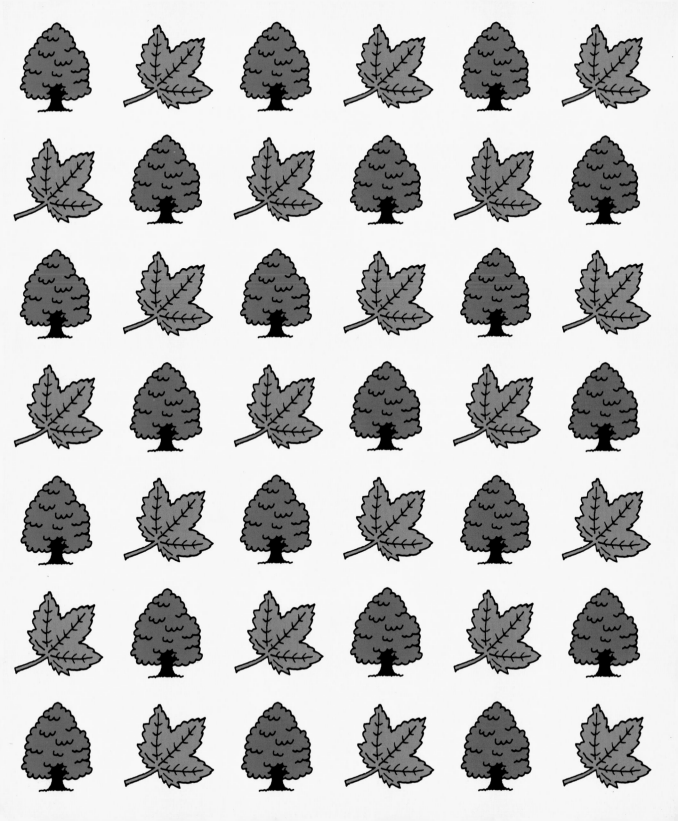